Parents

"They're Driving Me Crazy!"

By Kate Havelin

Consultant:
Martha Farrell Erickson, PhD
Director of Children, Youth, and Family Consortium
University of Minnesota

Perspectives on Relationships

LifeMatters
an imprint of Capstone Press
Mankato, Minnesota

LifeMatters books are published by Capstone Press
818 North Willow Street • Mankato, Minnesota 56001
http://www.capstone-press.com

Printed in the United States of America

Library of Congress Cataloging-in-Publication Data
Havelin, Kate, 1961–
    Parents: "They're driving me crazy!" / by Kate Havelin
    Includes bibliographical references and index.
    Summary: Describes typical relationships between teenagers and their parents, reasons for conflicts, and strategies for improving relationships.
    ISBN 0-7368-0285-1 (book). — ISBN 0-7368-0295-9 (series)
    1. Parent and child Juvenile literature. 2. Parents Juvenile literature. [1. Parent and child.] I. Title. II. Series.
    HQ755.85.H387   2000
    306.874—DC21   99-29807
                                       CIP

YA
306.874

Staff Credits
Kristin Thoennes, editor; Adam Lazar, designer; Heidi Schoof, photo researcher

Photo Credits
Cover: International Stock/©Scott Barrow
FPG International/ ©Ron Chapple, 17, 22, 29, 31; ©Jim Cummins, 9, 58; ©Rob Gage, 53; ©Telegraph Colour Library, 6, 12, 19, 33, 36, 49, 55; ©Arthur Tilley, 5, 16
International Stock/ ©Laurie Bayer, 14; ©Bill Stanton, 35
Photobank, Inc./ ©Bill Lai, 59
Photo Network/ ©Bachmann, 25
Uniphoto Picture Agency/ ©Jackson Smith, 41
Visuals Unlimited/ ©Jeff Greenberg, 43

A 0 9 8 7 6 5 4 3 2 1

Table of Contents

This book provided by a
grant from the
Family Resource Council
Merced County
Office of Education

Chapter Overview

Many teenagers fight with their parents.

Teens often feel their parents control their life.

Fights happen in all kinds of families.

Family fights can make teens feel bad.

Family fights can make teens physically sick.

Chapter 1

Home Is Where the Fights Are

Beth Gets in Trouble

I can't believe my parents are mad at me again. Sometimes it seems like all they do is yell at me. Today I called my friend Terri when I got home from school. We had a lot to talk about. I kind of forgot to look at the clock. I didn't start my homework. And I guess I forgot to walk the dog.

When my dad came home, he blew up. It's not my fault the dog peed on the rug. But my dad and mom are mad at me. They said I can't call any friends for one week. I ran to my room and slammed the door. My life is horrible.

What Is There to Fight About?

Teens often feel they don't have any control over their life. Parents decide many important things that shape the life of teens. Parents decide where the family lives. They might choose what school their teens attend. Sometimes they choose their teens' clothes. Some parents even try to pick their teens' friends. It is parents' job to care for kids, but sometimes it seems they care too much.

Family fights are common for teenagers and their parents. Parents shout orders. Teenagers slam doors. The fights may be about school, clothes, or money. They may be about household chores or friends. But often, there are bigger reasons behind the battles.

Teens need parents, but they also need some freedom. Young people need privacy and time away from family. Teens need to decide things for themselves. They want to pick their own clothes. They want to choose their own friends or maybe to select their own classes. Yet many parents insist they know what is best. These conflicts often lead to fights.

Parents: "They're Driving Me Crazy!"

Many times teens have mixed feelings about their parents. Most teens love their parents. At the same time, some teens hate the way parents treat them. It's hard to be both loved and punished by the same people.

All Kinds of Families Fight

Fights happen in many different kinds of families. Some teens live with a mother and a father. Some live with one parent. Others live in step families. Some teens don't live with any parents. Instead, a grandparent, aunt, or uncle may be in charge. No two families are alike. However, most have problems to solve.

This book can help teens understand themselves. It also can help them understand the adults in their life. In this book, the word *parent* means any adult who is responsible for children or teens.

Teen Talk

"Sometimes I think my mom is so cool. Other times, I can't stand the sight or sound of her."
—Mick, age 16

Two Families Try Blending Their Rules

Sam's parents got divorced when he was five. Now Sam is in high school. Last year his mother remarried. Sam and his mom live with her new husband and his two daughters. Sam's step-dad, Roger, is very strict. Sam's mom and Roger try to treat all three kids the same. But Sam feels he ends up being punished more.

Last week, Sam stayed out an hour past curfew. Roger was furious. He took Sam's car keys. Now Sam is not allowed to drive for a month. All Sam can think about is turning 18. He cannot wait to live on his own.

Stress Hurts Kids

Family fights can make teens feel bad. Teens might get physically sick because of the anger and tension. They might not be able to think about school or work. Some teens do not talk with anyone about the fights at home. They keep their anger and frustration inside them. Keeping tense feelings inside can make people feel worse.

Points to Consider

Do you and your parents fight? If so, what kinds of things cause your family fights?

Make a list of what your parents do for you.

Now make a list of what you do for your parents.

How can you help your parents understand what it's like being a teen?

What can you do to understand your parents better?

Chapter Overview

Attaching, individuating, and renewing attachment are part of a natural cycle for children and their parents.

When babies and children learn about love and acceptance, they attach.

When teens become more independent, they individuate. There are healthy and unhealthy ways for teens to individuate.

Parents and children usually renew their attachment after children leave the family home.

Chapter 2

Why the Fights Happen

Teens and their parents fight for many reasons. Most of those reasons have to do with teens becoming independent. Teens become independent because it is a natural part of growing up.

A Natural Cycle for Families

Most families go through three stages while the children are growing up. The stages include:

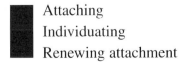

Attaching
Individuating
Renewing attachment

Individual families go through these stages at different times. Each member of the family can help the process go smoothly. Likewise, individual family members can make the process more difficult.

Attaching

The attaching stage is when most children learn about love and trust in relationships. These are the years when a strong bond usually develops between parents and children. This bond begins developing at birth and continues throughout life. It is especially close and important during childhood. When children feel the love and acceptance of their parents, they feel safe and secure.

Teenagers and two-year-olds have something in common. They both want independence. But they both need some parental guidance.

When children are very young, they want to be near their parents most of the time. As they get older, they feel confident enough to spend more time away from their parents, perhaps off at school or on the playground. However, they still need to know they can always count on their parents for love, comfort, and support.

Sometimes parents must express displeasure with children. This usually happens when kids disobey the rules of the house or do something unsafe. Children whose parents express anger in a healthy manner still feel loved. However, some children worry that they will not be loved if they disobey their parents. Parents should reassure children of their love, even during angry moments.

Mari Wanders Away

Four-year-old Mari and her father are at the shopping mall. Her father, Ron, is looking at a sale rack. Mari sees a piece of tinsel from a holiday display several feet away. She walks to it and picks it up. Mari sees more tinsel scattered around the store floor. She sets off to gather it up.

Ron is discussing the discounted prices with the sales clerk. He glances down to check on Mari but doesn't see her. Ron's eyes quickly scan the section of the store in which he is shopping. He sees Mari across the aisle in another section, bending down to pick up tinsel.

Ron sharply calls to Mari as he walks over to her. He angrily explains that Mari must stay close to him when they are in the mall. He tells Mari that she could get lost. Ron then explains how sad and scared he would feel if she were lost. Ron gives Mari a big hug.

Many Factors Can Affect the Family Attachment

Not all families have strong, secure attachments. The relationship between the two parents can affect the bond. For example, some parents are not close to each other and do not get along well. Children in these families might feel distant from their parents. In other families, parents are abusive. Children in those families might feel fearful or resentful rather than loved and accepted.

Other factors can determine how successfully a family will attach. The circumstances of a child's birth is one example. In some families, if a child was unplanned, it may take a while before the parents and child bond. An ill family member can affect the family attachment as well. For example, one sick child might get most of the parents' attention. The other children in the family therefore may feel less securely attached to their parents.

Individuating

Teenagers are on their way to being adults. This means that they must begin to define themselves as individuals. They will soon be making important decisions in the adult world. Therefore, teens must develop some of their own attitudes, beliefs, and behaviors.

Recent research suggests that healthy teens maintain a close connection to parents. Peers and independence become more important to teens at this time. Teens work hard to define themselves as individuals. However, staying attached to parents will help them find their identity in a smoother, more positive way.

Healthy Ways That Teens Can Individuate

Teens can individuate in many ways. One way is to wear clothing that differs from clothes they used to wear. Maybe they used to wear very colorful clothing but now choose all black. Another way is to speak differently from before. Some teens begin to use the language patterns that their friends use. These usually are healthy ways to individuate.

Some teens question their parents' beliefs and values. For example, they may begin to question why their parents vote the way they do. They might question why parents vote or don't vote at all. Another common area in which teens question their parents is religion. Many teens disagree with parents about having to go to worship services. Questioning beliefs is a healthy activity for teens.

A poll of 20,000 high school students showed:

47 percent admitted to stealing from a store
70 percent admitted to cheating on an exam
92 percent admitted to lying to their parents

Unhealthy Ways of Individuating

Some teens individuate in ways that might hurt themselves or others. They may begin to drink alcohol or use other drugs. They may steal or cheat simply to be different from who they were before. Some decide to become sexually active without thinking it through.

It's Hard for Parents to Let Go

Sometimes parents worry that their teens are growing up too quickly. Those parents may have a hard time with their teens becoming independent. Sometimes parents feel upset if routines or traditions that they value are disturbed.

Too Much Makeup

Allison and her mom were arguing in the kitchen—again. Her mom insisted that Allison take off some of her makeup.

"You are not wearing that much makeup in public."

"But Mom, this look is cool. Look in a magazine. I know you didn't wear your makeup like this, but times change."

Allison's mom replies that Allison is the one who has changed. She tells her daughter that she cannot leave the house until some of that makeup is removed.

Individuating is necessary if teens are to grow into healthy adults. Teens who are overprotected or who feel controlled may not grow confident in themselves. The individuating stage can be smoother if parents allow it to happen naturally.

Reattaching

Usually parents and their children renew their attachment after the young adult has left home. This closeness doesn't always happen right away. It may take weeks, months, or years. Family members often learn to love and accept each other for who they are.

Points to Consider

What kind of bond do you have with your parents? Do you consider it secure or insecure?

List three healthy ways teens can begin to individuate.

What can you teach your parents about the process of individuating?

Chapter Overview

Teenagers are between two worlds—the adult world and the child world.

It's hard to adapt to all the changes of growing up.

Teenagers are learning to see their parents differently.

Teenagers need to help parents treat the young adults differently.

Chapter 3

A New You Means New Rules

Your body and mind are developing rapidly. Your emotions, or feelings, are also growing and changing. Sometimes you may feel grown-up and confident. Other times you may feel overwhelmed by life. These changing feelings are normal for teenagers.

Teenagers sometimes feel stuck in a nowhere land. You are past childhood but not yet a grown-up. You still live at home with parents. You aren't as independent as you may want to be. Chances are, you still depend on your parents for an allowance. Your parents control the house. It might feel like they are trying to control you. Many teens feel that their parents don't understand them.

Today is Jana's 15th birthday. **Jana's Unhappy Birthday** Her mom baked Jana's favorite chocolate cake. Her younger brother even tried to be nice to her.

The family birthday party went fine until Jana opened her presents. The first gift was from her dad. The box looked big and beautiful. But when Jana peeked inside, she wanted to cry. Her dad's present was a plaid jacket. "It's so ugly!" Jana screamed inside her head. She could not think of anything nice to say. She just sat quietly, staring at the jacket she hated.

Her mom's present was another letdown. Instead of the shorts Jana had hinted at, her mom gave her ugly green shorts. Jana wanted to run to her room. When would her parents realize she can pick out her own clothes? Even though her parents wanted to make Jana happy, she felt upset. Her birthday was ruined.

Parents: "They're Driving Me Crazy!"

"I wouldn't have turned out the way I was if I didn't have all those old-fashioned values to rebel against."
—Madonna

Teens sometimes don't realize how hard parents actually try to please them. For example, Jana's mom remembered that a year earlier, Jana loved green. That's why her mom chose the shorts she did. This year, however, Jana loved the color black. Her mom had tried to please Jana without her even realizing it.

Parents Look Back on Your Childhood

Parents may miss the child you were. They may still try to treat you like a baby. Parents may worry they don't know how to take care of you now that you're a teen. They might feel they do not know how to protect you or control you. Sometimes parents get scared. They worry about teenagers using alcohol and other drugs. They worry about their teens driving cars.

Did You Know?

Teenagers and elderly people face the highest risk of feeling lonely.

Sometimes teens feel bad when they realize their parents make mistakes. When kids are young, they think parents know everything. Toddlers expect parents to know how to do and fix everything. Older kids see that parents are human. Parents make mistakes because they don't know everything. Sometimes they let you down. Sometimes they embarrass you.

The Wrong Pants—and More

My mom dresses so weird. She always wears this nasty old shirt and these pants that don't fit. They make her look fat. I've tried to tell her nicely to wear something different. But she doesn't care how she looks. Mom's clothes embarrass me. I wish my friends didn't see her wearing such stupid outfits.

Parents and Teens Need to Figure Out the New You

You and your parents need to accept the new you. Parents may still treat you like you're in third grade. Your job is to make your parents understand you are growing up. If parents seem stuck in old ways of treating you, you need to wow them. Show them you deserve respect, responsibility, and independence.

Points to Consider

Do your parents treat you like a child? If so, why do you think they do so?

List three things you can do to show your parents you are more mature than they think you are.

Do you think your parents worry about you? Are there good reasons why your parents worry about you? Explain.

How will being a year older make a difference in your relationship with your parents?

Chapter Overview

You have the power to control your own behavior.

Teens who are responsible usually get more freedom.

To get along with parents, learn what they are like.

Think of your parents as people.

Remember that parents are also changing.

Chapter 4

Understanding Yourself and Your Parents

Take a Look at Yourself

You actually have some power to stop family fights. You cannot stop all of them, but you can decide how to act. You can think about what to say. You can choose what things are worth fighting about.

More than eight million seventh through twelfth graders drink alcohol on a weekly basis.

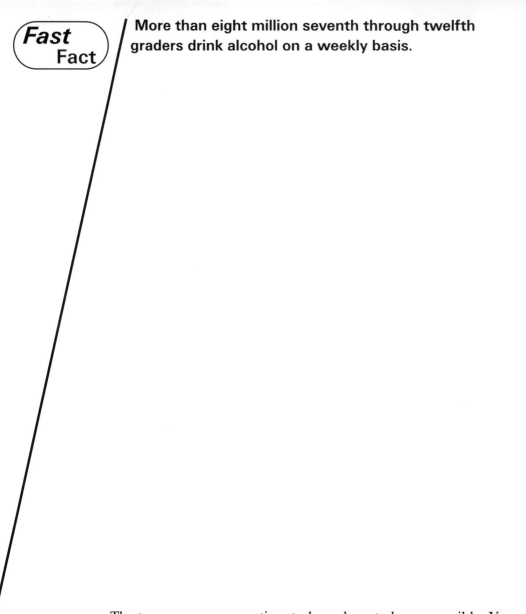

The teenage years are a time to learn how to be responsible. You will have to make important decisions in a few years. What will you do after high school? Do you want to go to college or vocational school? Do you want to get a job? Where do you want to live? You soon need to decide what you want.

The first step in learning what you want is being responsible. The first step in being responsible is accepting two basic facts:

Parents: "They're Driving Me Crazy!"

#1—Being grown up is not about drinking, smoking, or having sex.
Teenagers sometimes think growing up means drinking, smoking, or having sex. That's wrong. Yes, some adults do those things. However, being an adult means more than that. Being an adult is about being mature. Teens need to understand they cannot do everything adults do.

#2—Teens need to act responsibly before adults will give them more responsibility.
You may feel grown up. Your body may look grown up. But do you act grown up? Are you reliable? Do you accept the blame when you make a mistake? Being grown up means being responsible for your actions.

Fast Fact

Almost 90 percent of smokers start the habit before the age of 19.

So how responsible are you?

Take a good look at yourself. It's time to ask some tough questions about how you act. Be honest with yourself.

Do you:

Do chores without being nagged?

Keep track of time so you will not be late?

Follow the rules at home and at school?

Help around the house?

Say no to illegal drugs?

Drive safely?

Never drink and drive?

Think about others?

Respect yourself?

Show that you understand and can handle responsibilities?

Do what you think is right, even if your friends don't?

Stay calm when your parents get mad at you?

Grade Yourself

How did you do? Did you answer no to most of the questions? If
so, you are probably not acting responsibly. Think about it.
Parents worry about teens who do drugs, drink, or drink and
drive. Parents worry that those teens are not able to handle
freedom. Their worrying might keep you from having
certain freedoms.

Teens who answered yes to most questions probably are pretty
responsible. Chances are, you are ready for some freedom and
respect. Now you have to convince your parents that you
are mature.

A Few More Ideas

Even responsible teens get upset. It is important, therefore, to
know what upsets you. Sometimes writing things down can help.
The next time you and your parents fight, write down your
feelings. Or talk into a tape recorder, describing how you feel.
Once you are done, put down the letter or tape for a few days.
Check it out again when you have calmed down.

Parents spend an average of $149,820 raising a child to age 17.

Julie Gets a Diary

I used to wonder why my sister wrote in her diary every night. Now she lives in an apartment near her college. She gave me a diary for my birthday. I like to write down how I feel. It can be sloppy. No one checks the spelling. Sometimes I draw pictures of people I like or don't like. I like having a secret place to write down my feelings.

Take a Look at Your Parents

How well do you know your parents? Sure, you know their names. But do you know what they are like? What makes your dad mad? What makes your mom laugh? What does your mom do when she gets upset? Which parent is more likely to stay calm?

Know the Other Team

Your life will be smoother if you know what makes your parents tick. Understand them, and you can avoid some fights. You may learn some important facts that will improve your relationship with your parents. For example, do you know your parents' payday? That is probably the best time to ask for money.

Paul Runs Out of Cash

It's Friday afternoon. Paul wants to go to the movies tonight. He's broke. He spent his allowance playing video games.

As soon as his mom walks in the door, Paul asks if he can borrow $10 for the movies and pizza. His mom begins the same old lecture about making his allowance last the week. Paul just wants to scream, "Can I have the money?" Instead, he squirms and listens to his mom's speech. When she checks her purse, she hands him $5—not enough even to get into the movie, let alone buy popcorn. When he asks for more, she snaps.

Fast Fact

In a survey of teenagers, 41 percent of boys and 32 percent of girls said their fathers had an "explosive temper."

New Tricks to Try

To get to know your parents, try these tricks:

Think of your parents as people.

Pretend they are not your parents. Pretend they are strangers. Ask them what foods they like. Ask how their day went. Ask if they liked the TV show they were watching.

Learn what your parents were like when they were young.

Talk with your mom about her childhood. Ask your dad what he was like as a kid. Ask grandparents or other relatives to tell family stories. You may see a side of your parents you may not know. Their childhood may help you understand the way they are now.

Think of your parents as two separate people.

Is it easier to approach your mom than your dad? Why? Ask your mom to tell you more about herself. Then ask her to tell you more about your dad.

Things to Remember

Keep these things in mind as you try your tricks:

You are not searching for dark secrets.

These tips are ways to get to know your parents. You need to learn who they are. Then you can understand why they act the way they do.

Parents are changing.

Your parents are getting older as you grow up. Some parents get gray hair or wrinkles. Others gain weight. Most teens' parents are at the middle of their lives. That means half of their life is already over. Parents may wish they were young like you.

Parents worry about their parenting abilities.

Most parents are nervous about parenting a teenager. Many parents say they felt more confident parenting young children. Some parents admit that they are guessing at the best way to be a parent to a teenager.

Parents worry about money.

Parents have to pay for food, housing, clothes, and many other things. Many parents try to live on a budget. That means they make a plan for how much money they can spend. Sometimes unexpected expenses come up, like when the car breaks down. Money worries make parents tense. Parents may get angry when teens ask for extra money.

Parents worry about teenagers.

Parents are often afraid bad things will happen to their teens. Some teens use drugs. Some teens drink and drive. Some teens carry guns and are in gangs. Others have unprotected sex. All those behaviors can hurt teens. Some even die. Parents fear bad things could happen to their children.

Parents: "They're Driving Me Crazy!"

Parents are people, too.

Moms and dads have feelings. They can feel hurt, lonely, embarrassed, or unloved. In fact, they probably felt the same way when they were teenagers as you do now. To get along with parents, you have to treat them like people. You may not always like them. You may not agree with them. If you want them to respect you, however, you have to treat them with respect.

Points to Consider

Do you think your parents consider you responsible? Why or why not?

How can you help your parents trust you?

What do your parents worry about?

Imagine you are your parents. Would you worry about you? Why or why not?

Chapter Overview

Good communication improves family relations.

You need to talk and listen to communicate well.

It's important to find a good time to talk.

A family conference gives everyone a chance to discuss one problem.

Use the word *I* to tell people how you feel.

Chapter 5

Time to Talk and Time to Listen

Face it. Some family fights are still going to happen. But you can dodge some battles. There are two simple but powerful tools to avoid fighting.

Tool 1—Talk

Sometimes the best path to peace is communication. Let your parents know how you feel. Explain why you think they are not being fair. Be polite. Whines, insults, tantrums, or rudeness will only make things worse.

In a survey, some 500 family counselors agreed that the number one trait of strong families is the ability to communicate.

Tool 2—Listen

The only way things will improve is if both sides are open. That means you need to listen to what your parents are saying. Pay attention to them, and maybe they will pay attention to you.

Many teens feel their parents don't listen to them. Have you given them a chance to listen to you? If you aren't sure how, try these five tips:

Tip 1—Think About Timing

You need to learn when to ask parents for things. Timing is everything. Sometimes parents are too busy to listen to teens carefully. Parents may be stressed, worried, or mad. Ask them directly, "Is now a good time to talk?"

Tip 2—Have Family Conferences

Try having family conferences. The meetings can include parents, you, and siblings. Get everyone to agree to tackle just one problem. The topic might be the car, your clothes, schoolwork, household chores, curfews, or other issues. If the conferences work, they should be ongoing.

I'm so mad. My parents want me home by 10:00 on Saturday night. **Maggie Needs to Talk**
They are still mad because of my bad report card. When will they stop punishing me? I'm doing my best. Why won't they ever let me do what I want?

My friend Sarah has monthly meetings with her parents to talk about stuff. Maybe that would help my family. It couldn't hurt. I am going to ask my parents if we can have a family conference. Maybe my brother wants to talk about curfews, too.

Tip 3—Use the word *I*

Use the word *I* instead of the word *you* to let people know how you feel. People are less defensive if you focus on you, not them. Begin sentences with "I wish . . ." or "I feel . . . ." Avoid sentences that begin "You make me mad . . ." or "You do this . . . ."

"Oh—I listen a lot and talk less. You can't learn anything when you're talking."—Bing Crosby

Maggie's Family Conference

"Mom, Dad, Joe, thanks for agreeing to this family conference. I want to talk about curfews. Let me tell you what I think, and then I will listen to you, okay?"

"I know my report card was not so great. But I really am trying in school. And I deserve to have some fun with my friends. I think I am old enough to stay out until midnight on Saturday. I promise to study two hours each week night and on Sunday. Does that sound fair to you? Now, I will be quiet and listen to you."

Tip 4—Say It in Writing

Some teenagers just cannot talk with their parents. It is possible, however, to communicate without talking. Try writing them a letter. Take your time writing it. You can say exactly how you feel. Explain that you're upset but that you want to make things work. Reread the letter a few times before giving it to them.

Tip 5—Ask Parents to Think Like a Teen

Ask your parents to think about the stress of adolescence. At first, they may snort and say that you have it easy. Then ask them to pick any age they would like to be. Chances are, they won't want to be a teen again.

Sometimes parents get caught up in their adult world. They might think kids have no pressures. Your job is to show your parents what it is like to be a teen today. Let them see what your world is like.

Points to Consider

Do you and your parents really talk? Explain.

Do your parents listen to you? Do you listen to them? Explain.

How might you improve your communication with your parents?

What are the topics you and your parents fight about most often?

Try writing a letter to tell your parents how you feel. (You do not have to give it to them.)

Chapter Overview

One of the best ways to get along is to compromise.

Make a deal with your parents so both sides get something they want.

Look for a hobby or common interest with a parent.

Create a new tradition—something positive to do with your family.

Say three powerful words—I am sorry—to turn a situation around.

Chapter 6

Meet in the Middle

You and your parents will probably get along better if everyone compromises. Each side needs to give in a little. You'll get some of what you want. Your parents will get some of what they want.

Play Let's Make a Deal

You and parents can be partners. Think about what you, your mom, and your dad each wants. Do your parents want you to spend more time at home? Are you desperate for the car on Friday nights? Once you are clear on what's important to everyone, try to make a deal. For example, you can agree to spend each Thursday night with the family. In exchange, your parents agree to lend you the car on Fridays.

Make a Contract

Put your deal in writing. It doesn't have to be fancy. You should include what you and your parents have promised to do differently. You might also want to write what will happen if someone breaks the deal.

Rafael Signs a Contract

Dear Mom:

Please consider this a contract between you and me.

I agree to:
Pick up my room once a day
Vacuum the living room once a week
Wash the dinner dishes every night
Be in bed by 11:00 p.m. on weeknights

In exchange, you agree to:
Stay out of my room unless I'm there
Let me drive the car most Friday nights
Let me stay out until 11:30 p.m. one weekend night
Let me sleep in until 11:00 a.m. one weekend morning

If I break my part of the deal, you can restrict my privileges until we discuss what happened. If you break your part of the deal, I will not be expected to meet my requirements until we discuss what happened.

Love,

Rafael   _____(signed and dated)_____

Mom   _____(signed and dated) _____

Today, the average child spends forty percent less time with his or her parents than children in the 1960s did.

Realize That Some Parents Are Unfair

Sometimes parents want to control or protect their teens too much. Those parents do not want their children to become too independent. Those parents refuse to give their teens privacy or freedom. Some parents want to control everything their kids do. It is hard to have parents who are too strict. Teens may not be able to reason with overprotective parents. Those teens should talk with a trusted adult for advice.

Set Aside Tough Issues and Find Common Ground

Maybe you and your parents can't agree on some big issues. However, you can probably find something to agree on. Look for a hobby or sport you both enjoy. Watch a ball game together. Try a community education class together. Meet somewhere for a snack from time to time. Find time for parents so they can see how you are changing.

"Family jokes, though rightly cursed by strangers, are the bonds that keeps most families alive."
—Stella Benson

Start New Traditions

Try to break the pattern if you and your parents fight too much. Start a new tradition. Think of something that you like to do and get your family to try it. Ask your family to bake homemade pizza once a week. Set a movie night and then take turns choosing videos. Make ice cream sundaes each Sunday. Plan family time together to take walks, watch movies, or rake leaves.

Keisha Compromises

Keisha is a junior, busy with classes, soccer, and friends. Her parents work full time and are tired and stressed by evening. They often snap at Keisha when she asks for something. And they resent the way she never spends time with them. They want her to spend all day Sunday at home. That is the time Keisha goes to the mall with friends.

Both Keisha and her parents agreed to compromise. Now, Keisha spends Tuesday nights and one Saturday a month with her family. In exchange, she gets permission to go to the mall every Sunday.

Apologize

Sometimes the best way to compromise is to admit you are wrong. *Sorry* is a powerful word when you mean it. Use it sincerely. You may be surprised at how saying you're sorry, and meaning it, can make a difference.

Points to Consider

Try making deals with your parents. Think of something you are willing to give your parents in exchange for something you want.

What is one activity you and your parents could enjoy together?

Do you make time to be with your family? If not, why not?

How do your parents react when you say you are sorry?

How do you react when your parents say they are sorry?

Chapter Overview

Sometimes it helps to talk with someone outside your family about family problems. Counselors, psychologists, and religious leaders are all trained to listen and offer advice.

Parents are often stressed by their own problems.

Teens cannot solve their parents' problems.

Some parents refuse to get help for their problems.

You can get help for yourself. You can find someone who will listen.

Chapter 7

When Nothing Works

What do you do when nothing seems to help? You tried to compromise. You said you were sorry, but your parents still will not budge. Tackle the problem another way.

Ask Someone Else for Advice

You may want to ask another trusted adult what to do. Talk with an aunt or uncle, a friendly teacher, or a coach. Be clear about what you want. Do you want them simply to listen or to offer their advice? Do you want them to talk with your parents? Be clear with them to prevent further problems.

"Family quarrels are bitter things. They don't go according to any rules. They're not like aches or wounds; they're more like splits in the skin that won't heal because there's not enough material."
—F. Scott Fitzgerald

Josh Talks With His Uncle

Josh and his parents fight all the time. So Josh tries to avoid his parents. He feels miserable.

Josh tells his favorite uncle how he feels. It feels good just to be able to talk with someone. Uncle Bill listens quietly and then asks Josh some questions. Does Josh know why his parents are mad? Are they just mad at him? Or are his parents mad at each other? Are they mad about something entirely different?

Bill's questions help Josh see his family more clearly. Josh realizes his folks are angry with one another, not just with him. He feels a little better knowing that. Bill tells Josh that kids cannot solve their parents' problems. Sometimes, parents are upset about adult problems. Maybe they have problems at work or with their marriage.

His uncle suggests that Josh talk with a school counselor. Bill also asks Josh to talk with him again in a week. Bill promises not to tell Josh's parents that they talked.

Talk With a Professional

There are people who can help families in trouble. They are professionals whose job is to work with parents and kids. Your school probably has counselors. Their job is to listen and to offer suggestions about what might help students. You can ask to speak with a counselor at your school's guidance office. The counselor will listen to you. He or she might suggest you talk with another professional—a psychologist or family therapist.

A psychologist is trained to help people when they are upset. Your school may have a psychologist or may be able to refer you to one nearby. A psychologist may want to meet with you privately or together with your parents. Sometimes parents refuse to get help. You can still get help, however, even if your parents will not.

Other helpful people include religious leaders. Priests, ministers, and rabbis are all trained to listen and offer advice.

If you do not know where to get help, check the phone book. Most phone books list crisis hotlines within the first few pages. Or you can look under *Counselors* or *Psychologists*. Chances are, you will find many listings for people and agencies that serve families. You can also see the *For More Information* section at the end of this book.

Fast Fact More than a million American children are involved in parental divorce each year.

You Can't Fix Your Parents' Serious Problems

Things were so

Carmen Gets Help, But Her Parents Won't

bad at home that Carmen went to her school counselor. She told him she could not sleep at night. Her grades were dropping. She wanted to run away. Carmen cried when she talked with the counselor. He gave her some tissues and let her cry. He suggested she talk with a family counselor named Beth at the nearby community center.

Carmen met with Beth, who asked if Carmen's parents would also come in to talk. Carmen asked her parents to meet Beth, but they refused. They told her strangers did not need to know their problems. Carmen tried to explain that Beth was helping her. It did not change her parents' attitudes. So Carmen continued to meet alone with Beth.

Beth reminded Carmen that kids cannot fix their parents' problems. Carmen's parents are still angry. But Beth taught Carmen how to handle some of her parents' outbursts. Now her grades are getting better. She does not feel responsible for all her family's troubles. She can sleep again.

Some parents are stressed because of their own problems. They may be worried about divorce, language barriers, or alcohol and other drug abuse. Remember, you cannot solve their serious problems even though you may want to. And you are not responsible for their problems. Your job is to get to know yourself and to grow up. You need to learn how to take care of yourself.

Try not to worry about the cost of counseling. Your parents' insurance plans probably cover the cost. School counselors and religious leaders do not charge for their help. Some agencies charge only what a client is able to pay.

Points to Consider

Who would you turn to with a family problem?

What things cause stress in your family? What can you do to reduce that stress?

Do you know where the counselor's office is in your school? If not, ask a staff person or teacher where you can find it.

Chapter Overview

You are changing.

Your parents will always be your parents.

The fights can end.

You cannot solve your parents' serious problems.

You can always find help.

Chapter 8

Important Stuff to Remember

Whatever happens between you and your parents, you should remember some important points:

1. You are changing.

You won't be a teen living at home with your parents forever. Chances are, in a few years you will move out. Maybe you will get a job. Maybe you will go for more schooling. You will grow up and be on your own.

2. Your parents will always be your parents.

You will never have another mom or another dad. Kids of all ages need their parents' love. Parents need their children's love. It is worth the effort to try to get along.

3. The fights can end.

You and your parents may fight all the time now. When you are an adult, you'll probably get along better. It is easier to get along with people who do not control your life. Your teenage years can be very stressful for you and your parents. When you get older, many of the things you fight about will no longer be a problem.

4. You cannot solve your parents' serious problems.

You are not the parent. It's not your job to take care of the whole family. It's not your job to solve your parents' problems. You can be understanding, but your main job is to learn how to handle your own problems. That will help you now and later when you are an adult.

5. You can always find help.

Lots of people want to help you. There are teachers, counselors, coaches, and psychologists who will help you. Those people can listen to you. They can offer suggestions and help you handle all kinds of problems. You are not alone. Someone can help you.

Points to Consider

How do you imagine your relationship with your parents after you leave home and become an adult?

What can you do now to improve your relationship with your parents? What do you think they can do now?

Find a phone book and look up three numbers you could call for help with family problems.

Glossary

allowance (uh-LOU-uhnss)—money given to someone regularly

attaching (uh-TACH-ing)—the process of forming a close emotional connection to someone

communication (kuh-myoo-nuh-KAY-shuhn)—the exchange of ideas, feelings, or messages between two or more people

contract (KON-trakt)—a formal agreement, usually written, between two or more people

emotion (ee-MOH-shuhn)—a strong feeling such as anger, love, grief, or happiness

family (FAM-uh-lee)—any group of people related by blood or marriage

independence (in-dee-PEN-duhnss)—freedom from the control of others

individuating (in-duh-VIJ-oo-ayt-ing)—the process of becoming more independent and individual

parent (PAIR-uhnt)—a mother or father; can also mean a step parent or any person responsible for a child

psychologist (sye-KOL-uh-jist)—a person trained to help people with their emotional and behavioral problems

reattaching (REE-uh-tach-ing)—the process in which people come back together emotionally after a separation

responsibility (ree-spon-suh-BIL-uh-tee)—a duty or a job

stress (STRESS)—pressure

teenager (TEEN-ayj-ur)—a person between the ages of 13 and 19

therapist (THAIR-uh-pisst)—a person trained to help people handle physical or emotional problems

For More Information

Carlson-Johnson, Linda. *Everything You Need to Know About Your Parents' Divorce.* New York: Rosen, 1995.

Havelin, Kate. *Family Violence: My Parents Hurt Each Other!* Mankato, MN: Capstone Press, 2000.

Marshall, Brian. *The Teenager's Guide to the Real World.* New York: BYG, 1997.

Tener, Elizabeth. *Relationships.* Austin, TX: Steck-Vaughn, 1995.

Useful Addresses and Internet Sites

Alliance for Children and Families
1701 K Street Northwest, Suite 200
Washington, DC 20006
1-800-220-1016

The Children's Foundation
725 15th Street Northwest, Suite 505
Washington, DC 20005

Kids Help Phone
2 Bloor Street West, Suite 100
P.O. Box 513
Toronto, ON M4W 3E2
CANADA
1-800-608-6868 (in Canada)

National Council on Family Relations
3989 Central Avenue Northeast, Suite 550
Minneapolis, MN 55421

The Children's Foundation
http://www.childrensfoundation.net/
Tries to improve the lives of children and
those who care for children

Children's Defense Fund
http://www.childrensdefense.org/
Provides information about giving children a
healthy, fair, and safe start in life

Indiana University Center for
Adolescent Studies
http://education.indiana.edu/cas/cashmpg.html
Provides tools for teens to learn and practice
new and healthy behaviors

Family Resource Coalition of America
http://www.frca.org
Provides help in strengthening and supporting
families

Index

Index continued